Mel Bay Presents

Jazz Duets
TRUMPET EDITION
By Al Biondi

1 2 3 4 5 6 7 8 9 0

© 2005 BY MEL BAY PUBLICATIONS, INC., PACIFIC, MO 63069.
ALL RIGHTS RESERVED. INTERNATIONAL COPYRIGHT SECURED. B.M.I. MADE AND PRINTED IN U.S.A.

Visit us on the Web at www.melbay.com — E-mail us at email@melbay.com

Contents

About the Author..3

Al See Ya Later..4

Today's Special.. 6

After You... 8

Beagle Mania..10

Blues for Two...12

Rush Hour..14

Hot Tamale.. 16

Around the Clock...18

Good Morning Sunset..20

New York Blues...22

Let Us Play for Awhile.. 24

Close Shave...26

Al B's Dream..28

Al Biondi was born in Brooklyn, New York in 1957 where he hails from a musical family whose four generations of professional musicians span the last century. He has successfully led his own combo as well as a 17-piece Big Band since 1974 and continues to do so. He has studied with some of New York's leading instructors and, in turn, enjoys passing along his musical knowledge to the dozens of students he has helped to further their musical ability.

Al See Ya Later

Al Biondi

12/18
TOP

4

Today's Special

Al Biondi

6

After You

Al Biondi

Beagle Mania

Al Biondi

Blues for Two

Al Biondi

Rush Hour

Al Biondi

Hot Tamale

Al Biondi

16

Around the Clock

Al Biondi

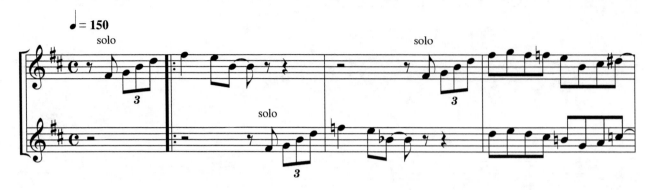

Good Morning Sunset

Al Biondi

straight 8ths

New York Blues

Al Biondi

Let Us Play for Awhile

Al Biondi

Close Shave

Al Biondi

Al B's Dream

Al Biondi